# THE ADOLESCENT ADULT

POETRY BY

# TAYLOR MOON

For all of us
navigating life's messy, beautiful middle
and daring to keep showing up
anyway

This poetry collection explores the contrasting yet interconnected experiences of adolescence and adulthood. The poems written in adolescence express a longing for the freedom and possibilities of adulthood, while those from adulthood reflect a nostalgia for the simplicity of youth.

The anthology captures the universal human experience of growth and change, highlighting our tendency to idealize what we don't have. It's a reflective journey through time, emphasizing the unique joys and lessons of each life stage. From heartbreak to fajitas to endless love and tight jeans, this collection travels through the life of one adolescent adult. Her name is Taylor Moon.

## ADOLESCENCE: AGES 13 - 19

## ADULTHOOD:AGES 20-30-SOMETHING

# ADOLESCENCE: AGES 13 - 19

## HOPE'S HORIZON

It's hope that guides me,
Gets me through the day.
Hope that my future may just be free,
All in the words that I may say.

There's always a light, shining ever so bright,
But I must always keep it in sight, follow its flight.

Life is all around, there in every sound,
Breathe it in, let your heart pound.
As long as you care, love can always be found.

Mirroring back, there's always something grand,
But don't rush to understand,
Rather, it's best to simply take a stand.

Raise your voice, make your mark,
Like a feather's gentle arc,
Drifting in the breeze, make your start,
As long as you care, you play your part.

**A CRAZED BEAT**

Your gaze lifts,
In an instant, recognition shifts.
For you've journeyed with me,
Through every change, every phase.

When our eyes meet,
No challenge, nothing can defeat.
What awaits is our shared glow,
Love as radiant as the sun's continued flow.

A single touch, a shared sensation,
Carries a universe of emotion, a quiet revelation.

In that moment, something shifts within,
With each passing moment, it deepens again and again.
To a melody that from the outset took part,
Echoing endlessly, the rhythm of my beating heart.

**WORDS UNSPOKEN**

So much I wish to convey, yet you remain distant,
Your attention elsewhere, our moments inconsistent.

I long to share my thoughts, my fears, my cheer,
But your presence is elusive, never quite near.
My concern for you is deep, more than you might perceive,
Yet this chasm between us, I can hardly believe.

It feels as though miles stretch within a single room,
Your indifference looming like impending doom.
I question if your heart truly aligns with mine,
Seeking clues, some sign, to understand your design.

Answers dodge me, hidden in your silent gaze,
I yearn for your words to clear this bewildering
maze.

In solitude, I ponder, this shouldn't be my plight,
Yet I'm drawn to you, hoping to ignite your
light.

Alone, I stand amidst the shadows of our
tale,
While you move freely, leaving me to pale.
The unknown stretches vast, a relentless
sea,
I'm lost, struggling to be free.

If only my company were what you
sought.
Perhaps, in our shared moments,
understanding may be caught.

**WHAT WAS**

The echoes of our conversations linger,
As I yearn for you, beyond the barrier thinner.
The memory of our singular embrace,
Intertwined with the whimsy, we'd chase.

In stillness, I remain, a vigil of hope and plea,
Wishing for the moment you'd rediscover me.

For all that was you, remains etched within,
A relentless longing, a fervent din.
Can't you discern, in this silence, my call?
This heart refuses to acknowledge the fall.

I reminisce about our nocturnal whispers,
Even discord, now just hazy flickers.
The solace of your touch, a missing balm,
For all that was you, I carry a mournful calm.

Can't you sense my unwavering plea?
In the grip of the past, I'm unable to flee.

I dream of a morrow where you retrace your steps,
To fill the void where solitude weeps.
Yearning for the casual greeting, the start of a tale anew,
To mend the emptiness with the essence of you.

I miss the depth in your gaze, the shared trivial delights,
The comfort of your embrace, through the endless nights.

If only you could unravel…

The words unspoken, the sentiments veiled,
Would the truth have altered the ship that sailed?

**THE TURN AROUND**

He promised a call within the hour,
So you pause, giving him the power.
A simple task, a brief shower,
Yet silence extends, the mood turns sour.

Deception is a game played far too wide,
In the end, it's you who decides to confide.
Claims of this, claims of that, a convenient concealment,
While you sift through distractions, hope in impeachment.

As minutes morph to hours unreturned,
The sting of neglect quietly burns.
Tears threaten, emotions churn,
In the silence, painful lessons soon to be learned.

Truth is unveiled in digital frames,
No this or that, just empty games.
Betrayal is sharp, as sorrow claims,
The realization of other names.

Choosing to rise from this painful seat,
Refusing to be tangled in deceit.
The truth is clear, no need to repeat,
Walking away, reclaiming my beat.

In a world rife with lies and masquerade,
The cost of trust becomes heavily weighed.
But in this moment, a decision made,
To seek a path where truth will not fade.

**SEARCH AND FIND**

Is it worth the absence, the void when you're away?
Thoughts linger on the divergence, our paths astray.

Yet, in this tapestry, each has a thread to weave,
Some are in solitude; others wait in the hope they believe.
Meaning transcends the obvious; deeper it lies,
In the quiet moments, beneath the open skies.

Around me, the world seems void of warmth, faces drawn,
Yet, within this shifting chapter, a new dawn is born.

Comfort zones falter as hope gently pulls,
A whisper to move forward, despite the lulls.
Why do I hesitate when optimism calls?
The journey to self demands breaking walls.

The end arrives, yet your shadow lingers on,
Eclipsing my light, my clarity gone.
Release me, let me find my place in the sun,
To discover myself, to become undone.

Navigating this self-revelation is no easy feat,
An identity obscured, like a river's retreat.
The struggle like a dam under strain,
Holding back the flood, amidst the rain.

## ROJO CHANGE

You said you'd always be there.
However, you just continue to change ~~the color of your hair.~~

Your core is pure, yet turmoil just lies there.
"Conform," they say, yet is that truly fair?
In this ~~charade~~, do you even care?

Choices aren't yours, trapped in a role,
In silence, you play, l o s i n g   y o u r   s o u l .
Speak up, break free, don't let them control.
Find your ~~voice~~, in utter defiance, be whole.

Calls go unanswered, you chase what's fleeting,
Leaving me here, heart silently beating.
Their presence, ephemeral, l a c k i n g   i n   m e a n i n g ,
I wish you'd see beyond the deceiving.

Embrace your essence, let the false go,
Stand firm, ~~resist~~, let your true self show.

Forget the new; let the genuine grow,
~~Remain unchanged~~, amidst the ebb and flow.

## REDEFINING HOPE

A gap wide, filled with quiet despair,
Holding onto hope, thin as air.
Time marches on, widening the space,
Leaving behind a longing trace.

Yet, in the stillness, hope flickers bright,
A wish for love to set things right.
Reaching out, a silent plea,
For a chance to mend, for you and me.

In the quiet, a gesture, a sign,
Hoping for a bond to redefine.
Longing for a moment, for hearts to mend,
Believing it's not the end.

**FLIPPED HATS AND TIGHT JEANS**

They always know the way,
To lift my spirits high, with just a smile, I begin to sway.
Like a warm, embracing hug, a comfort so dear,
I find myself wishing to keep you always near.

Fate had a hand in crossing our paths, so true,
In this vast odyssey of life, I found a companion in you.
This season, perhaps, is meant to teach us why,
Without your laughter, the days would simply pass by.

Tonight, you'll be the star in my sky of thoughts so bright,
Hoping that this connection, this bond, we'll always keep tight.
You, with your easy charm and those tunes that never bore,
In this world of give and take, someone I adore.

Vibe your own, a blend of chill and kind,
Each laugh you share brightens my mind.
Let's vow now, our link will never fray,
Through every twist and turn, side-by-side, we'll stay.

## DISTANCE

A vast expanse stretching far and wide,
A silent testament to the space between, where
our memories reside.

Each night, as I surrender to slumber's gentle tide,
I yearn for your presence, a wish I cannot hide.
To awaken with you in the dawn's early light,
For in your embrace, all fears take flight.

Once adrift in a sea of vast uncertainty,
My heart's compass lost,
You, I stumbled upon, and no longer felt the frost.
My tangled thoughts, once in turmoil, were tossed,
In a moment of clarity, all doubts crossed.

Your words, a beacon, illuminate my mind's
darkest caves,
A soothing melody that my soul earnestly craves.
In the voice's echo, I find the strength to brave,
No longer cloaked in shadows, from this desire, I
won't waive.

This distance, though a challenge, cannot dim
what's been found,
For even across the miles, essence surrounds.
In every whispered breeze, the night's soft sound,
Love resonates; it profoundly rebounds.

The distance only reminds me of our existence.

**SALT AND FAJITAS**

Your presence brings joy, subtly profound,
In your company, even the dark days are sound.
When life's storms gather, and skies turn to slate,
Your laughter's a beacon, my heart's rapid gait.

With each shared smile, a promise is spun,
For countless tomorrows, under the same sun.
If only time could pause, in moments we thrive,
In the warmth of your friendship, I truly feel alive.

They say beyond the fence, the world's more bright,
Yet it's with you, the colors shine just right.
Together, we've laughed, our spirits in flight,
With you, fears dissipate into the night.

A mural of moments, both vivid and bland,
It's your friendship that makes me understand.
Joy isn't about the grandeur of the brand,
But in simple pleasures, like the salt in your hand.

Throughout our friendship, tinged with unspoken care,
A delicate balance, a connection rare.
Your unvoiced affection, a silent prayer,
In the simplicity of moments, we unknowingly share.

**HAPPINESS?**

You crave one thing,
I yearn for another,
Both aim not to smother.
Yet our bond teeters on a fragile wing.

Your joy brings mine,
My bliss, yours in kind,
Isn't that the truth we're meant to find?
A harmony so intertwined.

Our wishes don't always align,
Still, from each other, we can't resign.

We mirror each other's face,
Tied by the affection that we embrace.
Trying to put joy in its place,
A precious rarity in a wide-open space.

## PATTERNS

A constant change as the wind blows.
We grasp for steadiness, a lasting pact,
Yet, in our hands, it shifts, an elusive fact.

Voices mingle, their words a charade,
Intentions veiled, in shadows, they degrade.
We seek a shield, a front to don,
Yet clarity's script remains unwritten, withdrawn.

Footsteps falter, then return with the dawn,
In the dance of absence, bonds are torn and then reborn.
And when the final curtain falls, silent and gray,
Tears are shed, understanding gone completely astray.

Imperfection is the canvas of our existence, stark and true,
Amongst the flaws, some moments stick like glue.

Steering clear of the paths that lead us astray,
Embracing the light and letting it guide our way.
Though the road may twist, with burdens fraught,
Surrender not, for each step is a battle fought.

In the quest for what's right, in the face of the deep night,
Stand tall, stand strong, keeping the end in sight.

**ANYMORE**

Indifference has settled in, a stark and unwavering stance,
Today might bring triumph; tomorrow is left to pure chance.

So, why do we cling to status, wealth, the material with such zest?
It stirs within me a tumult, a profound protest.

Claims of disregard are often voiced, yet seldom true,
For beneath the surface lie concerns of rank and view.

Recall the time, a pretense of aloofness in your guise,
Amid the empty revelry, no genuine ties.

Thus, I find no merit in further discourse, no reason to persist.
Why expend my words on a connection that simply no longer exists?

## CONSCIOUSNESS

I am a mess, you see.
Problems go beyond infinity.

Laughter and love seem temporary.
But nothing in life is dealt with fairly.

I cannot show,
The message that no one knows.

Would it even matter?
Or would it all just scatter?

Confidence is a must.
But can't you see I'm about to bust.

Fear is held inside.
Perhaps in life, I need more pride.

Strength is needed to go on.
Otherwise, it will all be gone.

SEIZURE OF SILENCE

Alone in the shadows, I navigate. Through the maze of confusion, I hesitate. Epilepsy's grip, such a heavy weight, In the hourglass of time, slipping through my hand, I never imagined I'd bear this plight, In the frame of adolescence, I stand, Lost in a world I struggle to understand. A disability casting shadows in the night. The whispers of friends, like grains of sand, Feeling isolated, longing for light, In the midst of darkness, I try and fight. Confusion reigns, yet I strive to see, Beyond the confines of my reality. Yet amidst the chaos, I long to be free, From the shackles of epilepsy's decree. Though the road may twist, and shadows loom tall, I rise from each fall, determined to stand tall. A beacon of hope, shining ever bright, I try to navigate this tumultuous sea, With courage as my compass, guiding me. Epilepsy may try to define, For within me lies a strength, I feel I am more than the limits it tries to confine.

## LET GO AND LET GOD

It's still there.
I say it throughout my prayers.
It reflects off the moon,
A change within it I see soon.

Cause I don't want to wait.
But if it leads to a new,
So many would want that fate.

It's a dove that must fly.
Detachment to a change.
It's love that will never die.

# ADULTHOOD:
# AGES 20-30-SOMETHING

## EMPTY PAGE

I was ready. I sat down with purpose. Ready to write.
Blank canvas and ideas swirling. So clear, so bright.
Pen in hand and journal open wide,
But when pen came to paper, my thoughts seemed to hide.

Words that once easily flowed now trapped.
Completely inaccessible.
My mind scrambled, a complete mess.
Writer's block, painful distress.

I tried to focus, to pause, to find my groove.
But, my thoughts refused to move.
I screamed in anger, almost trying to break the spell.
Still, nothing came. Only an empty, blank shell.

Eyes closed. Deep breath.
Trying to push aside this feeling. Almost like death.
I felt I had nothing to offer. If only I had been softer.
Eyes closed. Deep breath. I reminded myself this was just a phase.
A moment alone and the words would soon come in waves.

In that moment, eyes closed, and I found a sliver of peace.
Writer's block, its grip on me, slowly released.
Slow trickle, then a river.
Words with true meaning are soon delivered.

No longer filled with anger and pride. I decided to just be.
Eventually, the words would set me free.

## BOUNDARIES FOR THE SOUL

Deep within my soul, where love and pain entwine,
Grew a light of hope amidst the shadows of decline.
A tender sprout, born from a heart so fraught,
Seeking sunlight in battles long fought.

A mother's love, a tempest wild and deep,
In its wake, secrets that shadows keep.
Her laughter, a melody in the air,
Her sorrow, a burden much too heavy to bear.

From the cradle of care to the storms of youth,
I treaded the waters of painful truth.
In her eyes, a dance of flames and ice,
A love so pure, but at an unbearable price.

With every sip of sorrow, she chose to drown,
A piece of my childhood silently worn down.
Yet love, a resilient, undying flame,
Burns for her in spite of all the pain.

Deep within my soul, I finally drew a line,
Not to divide, but to lovingly define.
Boundaries, not walls, I chose to build,
In the hope that broken spirits just might be healed.

For in setting these boundaries, not rigid, but kind,
I sought not to leave, but myself to find.
To love her, yet not the chaos embrace,
To walk beside, but at my own pace.

Each boundary set, a step toward the light,
A journey of healing, of reclaiming my right.
To breathe, to grow, to dream, to be,
To love her, yet first and foremost, love me.

Where pain and love grow,
There lies a strength that only the heart knows.
To set a boundary is not to sever,
But to nurture the soul, for now and forever.

## ALONE. FUCK. WORLD.

I'm so **alone** in this world. There's all those bullshit quotes saying that I am not.
They should **fuck** off. They never met me or showed compassion,
So I am **alone**, or someone forgot.

No matter where I turn in life, there is **despair**.
No matter which path I choose the result is the same.
No matter whom I turn to, they leave me.
No matter why I do certain things, it does not benefit.
No matter how hard I try.

Our world is **fucked** up. Head to toe.
Bleeding lies, installing fear and misguidance.
**Fake** is everywhere, blocking the truth from all those to know.
But for some reason, there is still pride in the **fakeness** that makes me want to hide.

Maybe it is my fault I am **alone**.
Maybe I am too hard on myself.
Maybe I want it this way and just can't realize.
Maybe I'm not meant to make connections in the forged world.
Maybe I just don't give a **fuck**.

I am **alone**. But I can't be the only one to feel this way.
Others must think as I do.
Feeling that **hope** has been drowned by blindness.
I am **alone**. But perhaps no one else is willing to say.

## COMPARISONS

Embarrassment
Judgment
Experiment
Irrelevant
Establishment
Environment
Development
Arrogant
Assessment
Punishment
Resentment
Harassment
We are all comparisons.

These words describe our lives.
Eating away at the flesh,
It continues and drives,
And we can't simply press refresh.

**MENDING**

Consolation
Affection
Connection
Reflection
Foundation
Compassion
Progression
Expression
Confession
Protection
Admission
Affirmation
We are woven through love's redemption.

These words, they shape our healing quest,
Soothing the heart that beats in and out of our chest.
With each tender touch, love's power is openly confessed,
In its embrace, we find our rest.

Though grief's shadow may linger and loom,
Love's light can brighten even the darkest room.
It binds and heals, dispels all of the gloom,
A gentle force, allowing us to bloom.

In love's soft whisper, grief finds release,
A path to peace, a sweet, slow crease.
With every shared tear, a piece of ease,
In love, we find our deepest peace.

**LOOK BOOK**

Yesterday. Today. Tomorrow. I'm sometimes scared to look.
What will be on TV? What will be in the news? God, I'm scared yet
entertained.

Right and wrong used to be just that. The facts.
NO LONGER. ██████████████████
It must be racist, scary, disgusting.

Are the lines blurred? Did they ever blend? OR WERE WE
ALL JUST BLIND FOR A BIT?

The streets are mean. ████████████
They're fueled by this unchecked, unbalanced machine. A wheel that
keeps on spinning. And spinning. Crushing those in its way.

There's a divide. One that was always there. We just ignored it. We
just looked past it. The wheel kept on spinning.
████████████████████████████████████████████

A new definition of right and wrong has been made. It's up to
me. To you. To us all. To keep redefining. But how? How
when those you love just won't listen. NOT TO YOU. To me.

They only listen to what's on TV.

Yesterday. Today, Tomorrow. I'm still scared to look.
But, I face the fear in hopes that we can learn and redefine this
chaotic book.

## WHAT COULD HAVE BEEN

My soul is not whole,
For I have given parts of it away.
I cannot get those back.
To the winds, they've been conveyed.

My sins create outcomes.
For which the sums, I will not always know.
But I am left with the guilt,
For which I wish I had not dealt,
And no longer felt.

I will never be able to give my entire soul to one,
Pieces have been placed within others.
The fun of an entire life together will no longer be that one journey.
Pieces are left upon covers of which I did not wish for.

My life will still go on.
I know that there is that someone.
My journey continues, despite the scars within.
Yet, I dread the echo of what might have been, had my choices not
woven sin.

## CALM OF THE MOMENT

The calm of the moment.
The creaking of the fan.
The soft jazz in the background.
The stillness of the house.

Someone press pause. For I know the moment cannot, will not last.
It always finds its way, becoming something of the past.

The sleeping dogs.
The once warm coffee.
The sunlit office.

Soak it in. Let it resonate.
As it will soon become the past.
It was well worth the wait.
Hopeful to resurface again. The future at last.
The future that then turns to the past.

The warmth of the room.
The comfort of the chair.

Hugging the body and mind.
Supporting it with each and every curve.
Life has never been so aligned.
Providing the moment well deserved.

The calm of the moment.

## CHOICES

Trapped, left alone,
Cold and forgotten,
To the bone.

All I have left is myself,
Myself and a shelf.

All the memories that once were sit right beside me,
They poke, prod, and invade my thoughts.
Pictures and objects all of those past memories,
Bad, good, loving, or hatred…
They are all there,
Stringing pain of all sorts through the strands of each hair.

I can't run away.
It will come back.
Can't throw away.
That's something that I lack.

Perhaps I should grow,
But I am scared.
Scared of what I already know,
But how am I to learn without my past and present paired.

Choices and questions are left to me.
Do I forget or move on?
Only if I knew what the outcomes were to be,
One's life is something you can't simply pawn.

If I choose to forget, what do I have to lean upon?
If I choose to remember, there is a chance I could progress.
Forgetting could only leave a well of questions to be drawn.
Remembering could only leave questions to address.

## NATURE'S EMBRACE

In the embrace of the forest, I found solace from life's relentless tests,
A year of storms had challenged me, yet in nature's heart, I found
solace.
Amidst the whispering leaves, serenity's song gently pressed,
A reminder of resilience, of the enduring spirit within my chest.
Though once my heart bore the scares of love's unreturned gaze,
I learned to see through the veil of rejection's fleeting phase.
From the ashes of despair, I rose, no longer in a daze,
Understanding that love's true form transcends these temporal
mazes.

With courage, I stepped into the light of new beginnings,
embracing the often dreaded unknown,
Each fall, a lesson, a stepping stone toward the growth I've shown.
No longer shackled by solitude's cold monotone.
I discovered strength in my journey, a resilience fully grown.

Through adversities, I've come to recognize my worth,
Beyond the shadows of a doubt, a new hope emerges forth.
In the warmth of genuine connections, I found mirth,
A testament to the enduring spirit of my rebirth.

## QUIET AFTERGLOW

Where new life breathes and stirs,
A mother's heart beats, boundless love for her child occurs.
Yet within her soul, a silent battle rages on,
A quest for self-love, in the dawn of motherhood's song.

Her body, a vessel of strength, a giver of life,
Now viewed through a lens of strife.
Curves that danced to the rhythm of creation,
Now scrutinized, lost in her own reflection.

She marvels at her child, love beyond measure,
In those tiny eyes, she finds her greatest treasure.
Yet mirrors whisper tales of change and loss,
Sounding out doubts, a burdensome albatross.

Nourishment flows, a bond so pure,
Yet with each embrace, her insecurities endure.
Physical aches, mental shadows creeping,
In quiet moments, silent tears she's weeping.

"Am I good enough?" the haunting refrain,
Amidst the joy, a persistent strain.
Her worth, undeniable in her child's embrace,
Yet obscured by her own clouds, difficult to trace.

Healing, the journey of reclaiming her light,
Is paved with patience, through day and night.
In the reflection of her child's adoring gaze,
May she find the strength, her spirit to raise.

For in this chapter of motherhood, raw and real,
She's everything and more, if only she could feel.
The fog of postpartum, thick and wide,
Cannot dim the love and power she holds inside.

**LIVING THE UNTOLD STORY**

Where did you come from?
I truly do not know.
You appeared when needed most,
A love soon diagnosed.

The giddiness, silliness, and fun,
You became such a light.
How could I not succumb?

Gazing into the depths of your eyes, a revelation so bold.
Never had I seen so clearly,
The pureness, chaos, support, and excitement.
Love became something so vivid, and I could not control.

To have, to hold…
All of that stuff.
We continue our journey,
Creating a story yet untold.

Writing as we continue to grow old.

## RADIANT ROOTS

In the heart of life's embrace,
A mother dreams of her child's grace.
In hues that blend, a radiant chase,
Blankets of heritage, a warm, wondrous place.

Within her arms, a cradle of light,
Where whispers blend in the silent night.
In every touch, a bond takes flight,
A journey of discovery, shining bright.

A daughter, a symphony of hues,
In her veins, stories old and new.
Her laughter, a melody that ensues,
In her, both worlds find their due.

Guiding steps through lands unseen,
Where shadows dance, and dreams convene,
A mother's love, a steadfast beam,
In her child, two worlds convene.

In her eyes, the stars align,
In her spirit, both worlds combine,
She's a beacon, a radiant sign,
In her heart, both roots entwine.

To her daughter, whispered in a sigh,
In every breath, beneath the sky,
Embrace the blend, let it fly,
In you, my dear, the world's ally.

Let the world seek your embrace,
In every step, in every space,
For in your soul, a boundless grace,
A fusion of worlds, a sacred place.

**THE CAVE**

In shadows deep, where echoes dwell,
Lies a cave, a personal hell.
A realm of solitude, veiled in night,
Yearning for just a sliver of light.

Yet within this darkness, a journey begins,
Seeking sparks, as hope subtly grins.
Miracles in moments, small yet profound,
In the quiet whispers, life's beauty can always be found.

Passions emerge, like stars in the sky,
Illuminating the path, as I dare to fly.
Grasping tightly to those dreams, while finding strength in the pain.

Emerging from the depths, confidence takes wing,
In the art of simply living, and the joy it can bring.
A friend, a mother, with love to impart,
Each act of kindness, a work of heart.

I find freedom, in the rush of air,
Cycling through life, wind through my hair.
Within the intricate weave of love, threads entwined,
Clutching steadfast, even when frayed and misaligned.

The cave, once a prison, now a pathway, a start,
To the light of self-belief, the warmth of a heart.
In the depths of despair, where I once caved,
Lies the story of how I fought, how I braved.

## LIFE'S RESENTMENT

Born from, a lineage shared,
A connection deep, yet uniquely bared.
Love at its core, a complex weave,
A story of us, hard to conceive.

Echoes of laughter, a shared melody,
Blind to the coming discord, a foreseen tragedy.
Their battles, unseen, waged in the quiet,
A specter haunting, an unending riot.

Reaching for them, finding space,
A presence missed, an empty embrace.
In their struggle, shadows cast,
A young heart bearing, wounds vast.

Paths taken in search of what was lost,
Choices made, not counting the cost.
Regret for roads, ventured in pain,
A bitter reminder, a permanent stain.

Through a new lens of time, now I see,
The weight of a crown, heavy, yet free.
Forgiveness, a gate, rusted shut,
The heart's deep scars, a narrative cut.

Steps toward change, a hopeful stride,
Yet, the past's scars, where they reside.
How to forgive, when memories persist,
Tugging at bonds, a twisty mist?

Our lives entwined, a complex thread,
Love and resentment, deeply spread.
A journey shared, through silent accord,
In the space between, understanding restored.

## DECEMBER'S EMBRACE

With pure grace, in December's gentle embrace, you came. My love.
My first.
A little miracle so tiny in my life. Beyond beautifully versed.
Your arrival brought out a whispered promise. A new day's soft
glow.

Your smile, such a radiant beacon, lighting up my darkest of days,
Just like sunbeams through a winter haze, setting my soul ablaze.
Every little giggle, each coo, every song sung, a tender verse,
Within your laughter, my world discovers its sweetest, most joyous
rehearse.

As you grow, your tiny teeth adorn your captivating, joyful grin.
A sight so pure; it's where my happiness begins.
Your eyes, little Buddha, like blue diamonds bright and clear,
Shine with innocence and wonder. They're the treasures I hold
dear.

Your sass, a charming dance, spirited and free,
A testament to your maturing self, bold and full of glee.
In each defiant stare, every playful, stubborn whirl,
I see the strength within you, my darling little girl.

It's with your presence that time stands still. Each moment is a
precious gift,
With you, my bebe, life's tapestry on an animated shift.
My first, my heart's true north, my shooting star so bright,
In your tiny, little hands, my world finds its most beautiful of lights.

Thank you for December's tender embrace.
For you my daughter, are more than just a dream that came true.
In you, I've found a love so deep it transcends both time and space.
You are my heart. My soul. My life. For all eternity.

**ABYSS LOVE**

A touch. A kiss.
So divine, we crash into an abyss.
Hopes and dreams from two become one.
Never once thought that this could be undone.

But when an abyss grows a floor,
Two become torn.
Questions arise that never did once before.

How does one fix an abyss?
Strip away the floor.
The two must reminisce,
And realize what they are responsible for.

Sometimes this question is never properly solved.
And from that, the two then dissolve.

But if they can account as to why,
An abyss was ever crashed into,
It is possible for the two to come through.

With just a touch, a kiss,
So divine that they crash into an abyss.
Their hopes and dreams become one,
And they strive so that this could never come undone.

**FOR ZIGGY, AND FUTURE SQUISH — WHENEVER YOU GET HERE.**

Growing up is weird. It's beautiful, messy, thrilling, and hard. This little book is a collection of those moments — from wanting to grow up too fast to looking back and wishing time had slowed down.

Ziggy, I hope you find pieces of yourself in these pages someday. And Squish, you too, whenever you show up.

May you hold on to the magic in every phase, even when it's hard to see it. Especially then.

Just hold on tight. It's all part of becoming.
And know, mom's always got you.

**EPILOGUE**

As the final page turns in this anthology, "The Adolescent Adult," we find ourselves reflecting on the mosaic of emotions and experiences that shape our journey from adolescence into adulthood. These poems, penned by Taylor Moon, are more than mere words.

We are reminded that life is a continuous journey of discovery. Each poem a stepping stone, a moment of understanding in the grand tapestry of life. We carry with us the lessons learned, the emotions felt, and the memories cherished.

To all who find themselves on the path from adolescence to adulthood, let this collection be a companion in your journey. May it inspire you to embrace every phase of life with its unique challenges and joys. And in moments of doubt or reflection, remember that you are not alone in this journey. The words are a testament to the shared human experience – a reminder that in every heartache, every laugh, every tear, and every smile, we are connected in our beautifully complex journey of growth.